BRITAIN IN OL

C000155608

SOUTHEND-ON-SEA

KEN CROWE

ALAN SUTTON PUBLISHING LIMITED

Alan Sutton Publishing Limited
Phoenix Mill · Far Thrupp · Stroud
Gloucestershire · GL5 2BU

First Published 1995

Cover photograph: (front) Southend Pier on
Regatta Day, 12 September 1900. (back) An
auctioneer in Southend, September 1900.

British Library Cataloguing in Publication Data.
A catalogue record for this book is available from
the British Library.

ISBN 0–7509–0809–2

Typeset in 9/10 Sabon.
Typesetting and origination by
Alan Sutton Publishing Limited.
Printed in Great Britain by
WBC Limited, Bridgend.

SOUTHEND MUSEUMS SERVICE

The service was formed in 1974, following Local Government reorganisation, and comprises the Central Museum (opened in 1981), Prittlewell Priory (opened as a museum in 1922), The Beecroft Art Gallery (opened in 1953) and Southchurch Hall, the latter and Prittlewell Priory being Grade I listed buildings.

Serving the people of south-east Essex, the museums collect, among other things, material relating to the history of Southend and the surrounding area. This collection includes a large pictorial archive which dates from about 1790. This is constantly being added to, and the museums service is always willing to accept donations of pictures. It welcomes the opportunity to copy images to add to the archive, which is actively consulted by the public – researchers, general public and students – and is often drawn on for local history displays and books such as this.

Supporting the work of the museums, and promoting their use by the public, are the Friends of Southend's Museums, formed in 1983. Their social and fund-raising activities have enabled the museums to increase the range and quality of services to those who wish to use them.

Contents

Unloading the barges at Southend, *c.* 1905.

Introduction

This is by no means the first pictorial history of Southend, and there are certainly several other histories of the town, either still in print or available from libraries. This one does not pretend to be a complete history and by no means would it claim to be the final word on the subject. Several areas of the town's history are not covered at all, or only in passing, such as education, religion and industries. Instead I have chosen to cover those areas for which good photographs have been available and which give an overall picture of Southend's history.

I have attempted to select photographs which have not appeared in print before. While this has largely been achieved, it has to be admitted that several of the photographs in the first section have appeared before in similar works, as have some, albeit very few, in the subsequent sections. This is owing to the paucity of alternative images to illustrate certain aspects of the town's history.

The photographs have come from a number of sources, some private, some public, the full list of acknowledgements for which appear on page 126. I would like to take this opportunity to thank all those people and institutions who have kindly allowed me to use their photographs in this book. The images are of three types. There are the family or holiday snaps, which usually feature people and are of a personal and 'immediate' nature. There are also the postcard views normally taken by professional photographers, many of whom would have been pharmacists by trade. These are normally of a very high standard, and I am very fortunate in being able to draw on the collections at Southend Museum of original glass-plate negatives used to produce some of the postcards. This avoided the use of printed cards, which, however good, are inferior to a modern print from the same negative. The third category of photograph is the official view, taken for record purposes, which include pictures taken by the local Council and press photographers.

It has been possible to select good quality images, including a large selection of previously unpublished views. These include images in sections 8 and 9 (which deals with the 1960s), showing two aspects of the town's history which have not been covered in previous works such as this. I make no apology for the fact that the former section is by far the longest in this book, and I hope that this will fill a much neglected gap in published accounts of the town.

The Essex Record Office holds vast amounts of documentary and illustrative material relating to the history of Southend, for example the minutes of the Southend Local Board (the predecessor of the Southend Council), and records of manorial courts and estates in the area, which are a most valuable source of information. At the Public Record Office can be found, for example, the

The photographer, G. Dawson, catches a lady about to go for a paddle in 1900.

Ministers' Accounts of the 1530s, which are very useful for the early history of Southend. Canterbury Cathedral archive keeps records relating to the holdings of Christ Church, Canterbury, which, in the Middle Ages, included Milton Hall.

Other major sources for local history research include newspapers (microfilms are available from Essex Libraries), directories and council minutes. Newspapers are a particularly rich source of information and can help to fill in details of events, help with gauging opinions of the time and are often the only surviving source of information about particular events. Southend Museums Service holds a large collection of photographs and, at the time of writing, a full catalogue of these is being compiled to make them more easily available to researchers. Altogether there are something in the order of 4,000 images of Southend and the surrounding area in its collections.

We must not neglect one of the most important sources: information which you, the public, own and which you generously provide to institutions such as museums. As I hope you will see from this book, a photograph of a scene, person or event is made so much more interesting and important when associated information is available – the people in the picture, the date it was taken, who took the picture and why, and what, in particular, it shows. I would ask those readers who have photographs of the area to allow them to be copied by such institutions as the museum. By this means, whatever happens to the originals, a copy will be available, in perpetuity, to future researchers.

Section One

EARLY DAYS

Modern Southend comprises the area covered by the medieval manors of Prittlewell Priory, Earls Hall, Temple Sutton, Milton Hall, and Chalkwell Hall (all within the ancient parish of Prittlewell), together with the neighbouring parishes of Southchurch and Eastwood. Southend did not directly derive its name from the south end of the village of Prittlewell, but from the fact that the original settlement of farms and fishermen's dwellings was at the southern extremity of the lands of Prittlewell Priory. The village of Prittlewell (lying principally within the manor of Earls Hall) and the monks of the priory had very little contact with each other. Unfortunately most of the medieval records of Prittlewell Priory have been lost or destroyed, so we have to rely on later documents for our information.

The early small settlement of 'South End' was farmed by tenants or leaseholders of the priory, the principal farm being Facons. The main means of communication was by river and the lane, later called 'Southend Lane' (and in more recent times Old Southend Road), leading to a jetty or landing stage at 'Stratende'. In the eighteenth century, with the discovery of oyster breeding grounds off shore, the settlement rapidly expanded westwards. . . .

The refectory, Prittlewell Priory (built *c.* 1200), during restoration *c.* 1918. The Cluniac Priory of St Mary's, Prittlewell, had been founded in the early twelfth century. In 1917 it was presented to the town by its last private owner, R.A. Jones, for use as a museum.

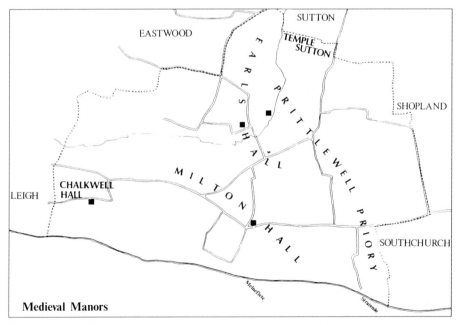

The two Domesday manors of Prittlewell and Milton Hall, divided, *c.* 1200. Prittlewell is divided between the priory and Earls Hall. Chalkwell Hall is formed within the lands of Milton.

Thames Farm, *c.* 1880. This farm, which in the Middle Ages had been known as Facons, lay at the heart of medieval Southend, at the southern end of the lands of Prittlewell Priory, which extended here down to the sea.

Milton Mill, from a painting by N.E. Green, *c.* 1860. Built as a 'new work' in 1299, a windmill stood on, or near, this site until the late nineteenth century. This was the lord's mill, at which tenants of the manor paid to grind their corn. The lane leading to the mill is now called Avenue Road.

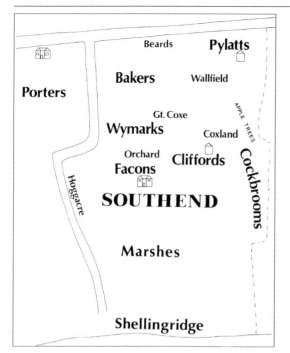

Porters

Beards

Pylatts

Bakers Wallfield

Gt. Coxe

Wymarks Coxland

APPLE TREES

Orchard **Cliffords**

Facons

Hoggacre

SOUTHEND

Cockbrooms

Marshes

Shellingridge

Medieval Southend. This map is based on information from documents describing the lands of Prittlewell Priory, following the dissolution of the monasteries. All of these lands later came into the possession of Hercules Arthur.

Milton Hall, given to the monks of Christ Church, Canterbury, in 959 by Agelward. A house had stood on this site since at least 1305, and probably long before. The site is now occupied by Nazareth House. This illustration dates from about 1890.

Southchurch Hall, before its restoration between 1927 and 1930. Although not strictly in 'Southend' until the turn of the present century, the ancient manor of Southchurch Hall is now very much part of modern Southend. Like Milton Hall, Southchurch had been granted to Canterbury in the Saxon period.

Another view of Southchurch Hall, taken before restoration. The present hall dates to the early fourteenth century, and there may have been an earlier building on the same site. The hall is an extremely fine example of a medieval moated manor house, and is now a branch museum of the Southend Museums Service.

Earls Hall. When Robert Fitzswein gave lands at Prittlewell for the building of a Cluniac priory, he and his family retained part of the manor for themselves. Following the marriage of Henry de Essex (Robert's son) to Alice de Vere the property eventually passed to the de Vere family, earls of Oxford, and hence, Earls Hall.

Daniel Robert Scratton, sitting on his favourite horse, Blackmore, and accompanied by two pair of hounds. This fine equestrian portrait was painted by Stephen Pearce in 1867. The Scrattons were lords of the manors of Milton Hall and Prittlewell Priory from the later seventeenth century.

The town of Prittlewell, largely within the manor of Earls Hall, following the creation of Prittlewell Priory. In 1238 the de Veres were granted permission to hold a Monday market at Prittlewell. The oldest houses clustered around the cross-roads and the parish church, which had been founded as a Saxon minster: many of these were demolished earlier this century. One of the houses, demolished in 1906, was called Reynolds, and the huge fireplace now forms a centrepiece in Southend's Central Museum. A house with a similar fireplace stood on the south side of the churchyard and was demolished in the 1950s.

Children waiting to attend the Penny Fund dinner for the poor, outside the Ship Hotel, January 1908. In the middle of the eighteenth century the small farming and fishing settlement of South End began to expand eastwards along the shoreline. A large house built for Mr Hain had by 1764 become the Ship Hotel.

With increasing trade and the discovery that oysters could be successfully bred off Southend, new properties were built to the west of Southend Lane. The first brick-built cottages, for the oyster fishermen, were constructed in 1767 by John Remnant, and called Pleasant Row. This photograph was taken shortly before they were demolished, in the 1950s.

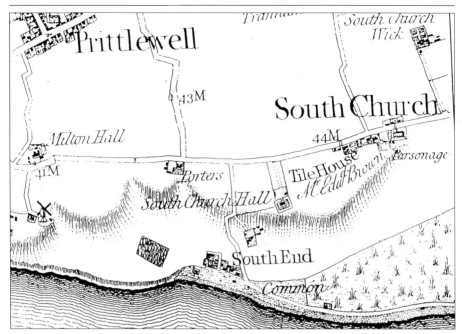

Chapman and André's map of South End, 1777. This extract from their *Atlas of Essex* shows the small settlement of South End, to the west of Southend Lane. On this map we can also see Porters, Milton Hall and the village of Prittlewell.

Southend, from a painting by J. de Fleury, *c*. 1790. It is painted from the site of the soon to be built Grand Terrace. In the distance, on the foreshore, can be seen a large white building, which is probably the Southend Baths. Also visible on the beach are some early bathing machines.

Royal Terrace, *c*. 1860. Built as the Grand or Capital Terrace, it was the centrepiece of the scheme for a 'new town'. At the beginning of the 1790s Daniel Scratton, the lord of the manor of Milton, sold three pieces of previously undeveloped land (on 99 year leases) to the west of South End, for the building of a new town. This terrace of houses was built by Pratt, Watts and Lowdoun (the lease later assigned to Thomas Holland) between 1791 and 1793. Behind the terrace was a row of stables with coach houses, called the Mews. Other parts of the scheme included the laying out of a north–south road, the High Street, and the road leading to the lower town, now Royal Hill, and the building of a library, hotel and a second terrace. The name Royal was applied to the first terrace, and other buildings, following the visit of Princess Caroline of Brunswick in 1801.

The Royal Hotel, built at the eastern end of the Terrace, *c*. 1860. It included a fine Assembly Rooms which a guide book of 1818 describes as 'handsomely finished, but . . . not regularly filled at any stated periods, though the company is always respectable'.

The Royal Library, part of 'New Southend', situated opposite the Hotel, *c*. 1860. The library had good reading rooms, supplied with London and provincial papers, and attendance in the evening was particularly good, owing to the raffles and other similar amusements.

Grove Terrace, when it had become the Lion public house, *c.* 1860. It was rebuilt later as the Grand Pier Hotel.

Grove House, 1900. This photograph was taken by G. Dawson when the house had become Grove House School. It stood at the end of Grove Road, now the site occupied by the Royals Shopping Centre. The house was demolished in 1935.

PIER AND SEAFRONT

By the end of the eighteenth century, the seafront from Southend Lane west to the hill leading to the New Town was quite built up. There was a mixture of private houses, shops and public houses. At the eastern end, beyond Southend Lane, was Prospect Place and the Theatre (from 1804); Vandervoord's great house stood at the corner of Southend Lane and the seafront, with his private landing stage or jetty. Further to the west were the Ship and Hope hotels and, at the western end of the seafront, the bow-fronted house of Mrs Stonard. By 1800 there were fifty-three houses and cottages in Old Southend.

There was no easy access from the river, however, to the growing watering place. After much heated argument, mainly concerning potential loss of private trade and fishing grounds, the landowners, fishermen and other major residents, led by Alderman William Heygate, agreed to apply to parliament for permission to build a pier at Southend. The foundation stone was laid in 1829 by the Lord Mayor of London, and the town's first, wooden, pier was opened for use in June 1830. The pier was extended in 1846, and replaced, in 1889, by an iron and steel structure which still stands today.

Southend Pier, 1860. This view by Secourable is probably the earliest photographic record of the pier. The original wooden structure was just half a mile long, and was opened in 1830. In 1846 the pier was extended to about 1¼ miles. A short way down the pier was the Octagon, a wide platform on which were held various entertainments. A canvas marquee was erected over this platform to protect the audiences from 'the scorching rays of the sun'. A horse-drawn tram service operated from the entrance to the end of the pier, passing through the Octagon. On the east side (left) of the pier was a small harbour and a landing stage adjoining the pier. Traders unloading goods on to the pier's landing stage had to pay a toll, as laid down in the First Pier Act of 1829. Prices included 1s. 9d. for a sedan chair, 2s. 6d. for a harpsichord and 5s. for a turtle.

Ken Crowe

will be signing copies of his book

SOUTHEND-ON-SEA
IN OLD PHOTOGRAPHS

At: HAMMICKS
11 The Royals, High Street,
Southend-on-Sea
On: Saturday 1st July
from: 12noon – 2.00pm

Southend Pier, 12 September 1900. The pier has always been popular, especially the new structure. Here it is seen thronging with people on Regatta Day.

The new pier, seen from the Hotel Metropole, 1900. The wooden pier was replaced with this fine iron and steel structure designed, by Sir James Brunlees, in 1889. It cost almost £70,000.

Enjoying a stroll on the new pier, *c.* 1890. In the distance, behind the pier, can be seen the scenic railway of the Pier Hill fairground.

The old pierhead from the new extension, *c.* 1910. It was soon realised that an extension was needed to deeper water, to accommodate more steamers. The extension was completed in 1898 and an upper deck opened in 1908.

Adam Seebold with his Southend Pier Orchestra in the bandstand, on the new pierhead, *c.* 1930. He came to England with his father's Chamonix Orchestra, and became musical director for the town. He retired at the outbreak of the Second World War.

The 'Prince George' extension, 1929. Properly called the eastern berthing arm, this extension was built to accommodate the ever-increasing number of pleasure steamers. It was opened on 8 July 1929 by H.R.H. Prince George.

Southend Pier has always been the town's most popular attraction. It was the world's longest pier, and pleasure steamers such as *Royal Daffodil, Medway Queen* and *Royal Sovereign* could be taken from the pierhead to Margate, Clacton, Walton-on-the-Naze, Yarmouth, Herne Bay, London, Sheerness and Ramsgate. In 1949 it was reported that over 1¼ million passengers had used the steamboats. Three million people used the pier in 1947; in 1949 this figure reached a record five million. An upper deck had been built on the Prince George extension, which became known as the Sun Deck. On the pierhead there were a number of restaurants, theatres, amusements and a small museum. This photograph was taken in about 1960.

Marine Parade looking east, 1897. The flags celebrate Queen Victoria's diamond jubilee. At this time most of the buildings along the seafront were still private houses, shops and pubs.

Another view of Marine Parade, this time looking west, *c.* 1905. Note the grassy area between the seaside and the buildings. This was one of the greens on which games used to be played and funfairs established.

Strutts Parade, Marine Parade, *c.* 1880. This small stretch of seafront took its name from its most famous resident, Major-General William Goodday Strutt (1762–1848), who moved to Marine Parade in 1824.

'Vandervoord's Pier Garden', 1900, by G. Dawson. The Vandervoords were Southend's major barge-owning family, who, in the late eighteenth century, had a large house built to the east of Marine Parade. It became the Minerva public house.

Marine Parade, looking east, *c.* 1900. The lines of horse-drawn vehicles are ready to take visitors on a round trip along the seafront. In the distance can be seen the Jolly Boys bandstand. This view is a detail from a 'real-photo' postcard.

East Front, Southend, 1900, by G. Dawson. This magnificent view of Southend shows
the seafront crowded with visitors. In the distance can be seen the new dome over the

entrance to the Kursaal, Southend's famous amusement park. Just to the right of this is the revolving tower.

Bathing machines, west of the pier, *c.* 1880. Bathing machines were an essential element of seaside life at a time when to be seen in a bathing costume would have offended public morality.

West Front, *c.* 1910. Taken from the new Pier Buildings, the view out to sea shows the Absalom floating baths. In the distance the new seafront road is being constructed.

Fruit stall outside the front entrance of the Kursaal, 1921. From left to right: Tom and
Frank Maywood (proprietors), Mick Heiser, Bill Hopcraft.

Ice-cream stall outside the Kursaal, 1921. The Minerva public house is in the
background. Bert and Mrs Baud are selling ice-creams, lemonade and Southend rock.
The fruit stall (above) and this one would occupy the same spot outside the Kursaal on
alternate days.

Jockey scales outside the Minerva public house, c. 1920. These were a very familiar sight on the seafront. When the fruit or ice-cream stall occupied this 'pitch', the scales would be moved to the other side of the road. From left to right: Mick Heiser, Frank Maywood, Bill Hopcraft, Tom Maywood.

'Happy Harry', c. 1960. Rev. George Wood began his evangelical preaching at Southend in about 1910. Crowds of holidaymakers and locals alike would stop to listen, heckle and throw pennies. He was subject to physical abuse on occasions, and retired in 1966. He died, aged 86, in 1974.

SOUTHEND AT PLAY

The growth of Southend as a major tourist resort was the result of its proximity to London, and the cheap rail fares at the end of the nineteenth century. However, Southend's amusements can be traced back rather earlier. In 1793 a play house was established in the town, first in a rented property, but soon in a building at the eastern end of the seafront. From the theatre, to the west, on the sea side of the road, were several open grassy areas called 'the greens'. These greens, or at least some of them, were the sites of cricket matches and other sports, and, very frequently, of amusements, either fairly permanent or seasonal, at summer weekends. Pawley's Green, opposite the southern end of Southchurch Avenue was the most famous – or infamous – of these.

On Pier Hill stood, in the later nineteenth century, Southend's first major amusement park – the Pier Hill fairground. Towards the end of the nineteenth century the Marine Park was established at the eastern end of the town, later to become Southend's, and the country's, most famous amusement park – the Kursaal.

A section of Dutheit's panorama of Southend, showing the extreme eastern part of the town, *c*. 1825. It depicts the theatre built in 1804 and Prospect Place, to the right. A cricket match is taking place on one of the greens.

Pier Hill fairground, *c*. 1890. A fairground had been established on Pier Hill in about 1889, and remained there for several years until the building of the Hotel Metropole. One of the most notable rides was the 'Roly-Poly': 'a contrivance by which could be secured all the joys of complete seasickness, without the danger of leaving dry land'.

The Marine Park trotting track, *c.* 1904. In the early 1890s Bernard Wiltshire Tollhurst, a local solicitor and entrepreneur, bought up land at the eastern end of the town for the creation of a Marine Park and gardens. One of the principal features was this trotting and cycling track. The area is now covered by a housing estate, built in the late 1970s.

The Kursall, *c.* 1922. The Aerial Flight was among the earliest amusements at the Marine Park and it was one of the few elements of the Marine Park to survive into the 1920s. The photograph was taken from the top of the waterchute.

Barnum's Circus, on its way to the Kursaal, 1899. Seen in Southchurch Road, this street parade of Barnum and Bailey's show was reported in the *Southend Standard* on 27 July 1899.

Togo, the snake charmer, was a familiar figure in the Kursaal in the 1920s and '30s. He was just one of several performers managed by Gordon Stumpke.

'Chief Idulbulgo' at the Kursaal, *c.* 1930. Another of Gordon Stumpke's side shows, his 'native' warriors are said to have been workers from the East India Docks in London.

The Togo stand at the Kursaal, *c*. 1930. Gordon Stumpke's grandchildren used to play in the snake pit between performances!

The waterchute, probably the Kursaal's most famous amusement, was opened in 1921. It stood towards the northern limits of the park, near Woodgrange Drive. By today's standards no doubt very tame, it certainly drew the crowds in the Kursaal's heyday.

The Kursaal entrance and façade, c. 1903. They were part of the scheme of the Pyramidal Railway Company, which had taken over the enterprise in the late 1890s. To the right is the revolving tower. The bathing machines were a familiar sight here until the First World War.

The revolving tower, which opened in 1898. This was known as the Warwick tower after the managing director of the company which owned it, Mr William Warwick. It stood in the Britannia fun fair, adjacent to the Britannia public house. The tower, 128 feet 8½ inches high, was taken down in 1905. The passengers were raised to the top of the tower in a platform which revolved in a spiral from the ground.

The 'Jolly Boys', *c.* 1910. A letter in the *Southend Standard* of 9 March 1961 recalls 'the Jolly Boys on the beach, where one could sit or stand around and get the fresh air and sunshine and see a really first-class show'.

The Jolly Boys bandstand, Marine Parade, *c.* 1930. The Jolly Boys began performing at Southend in 1896. Apart from the beach concerts they also performed in the Marine Parade bandstand, and this area became known as the 'Jolly Spot'.

The Jolly Boys. 'On one occasion the troupe gained special distinction by winning second prize in a competition open to the United Kingdom for the most popular entertainment.' (*Southend and Westcliff Graphic*, 1917.)

Stevens and the Girls, Concert Party, 1926. These were all local girls, looking for the chance to enter show business. They also performed at the Jolly Boys bandstand. The girl seated on the left is Elsie, who married Jack Heiser.

Going for a sail in the *Britannia*, 1905. Standing on the far right is John Brooks, known as 'Ripper' (because of his skill at filleting fish). His brother, Ernest, had nine pleasure boats moored between the Corporation jetty and the Army and Navy public house.

Southend from an aeroplane, *c.* 1910. In the bottom right can be seen the old Castle public house, adjacent to one of the several greens along the seafront. Behind is the Kursaal, opened in 1894 as the Marine Park, but taken over at the turn of the century by the Southend and Margate Kursaals Ltd. The trotting track can be seen in the grounds. Just below the 'R' of Kursaal is the site of the revolving tower, now replaced by the helter-skelter in the Britannia fun fair. Running down to the beach from in front of the Kursaal is Prospect Place. Further to the west (left) can be seen the Jolly Boys bandstand. In the far distance to the north, near the top of the photograph, can be seen St Erkenwald's church.

Chirgwin's concert party, 1907. They played in the Happy Valley bandstand, at the foot of the cliffs, west of the pier. The Happy Valley was replaced by the 'Floral Hall' between 1920 and 1921.

The heaviest man in the world! Dick Harrow weighed 30 stone (some reports say he weighed 40 stone) and was a major attraction at the Kursaal. He is pictured here in Alexandra Street. Behind him a man holds a card advertising the chair in which Dick is sitting.

The children's playground, *c.* 1930. Originally opened in the mid-1920s, in recent years it has become known as Peter Pan's playground.

The Floral Hall, *c.* 1930. It was built in 1920, but not called the Floral Hall until 1921. It was a replacement for the Happy Valley bandstand where Chirgwin and his players had performed (see previous page). The hall was destroyed by fire in August 1937.

Riding donkeys, *c*. 1930. There have been donkeys in Southend from the late nineteenth century, when they were used to drive carts as a form of taxi service. Some were probably always used for giving children rides along the seafront.

The Kursaal Flyer, *c*. 1960. Perhaps the most famous float of the Southend carnivals was the Kursaal Flyer, built in 1951. It appeared in carnivals and processions all over the country. The Southend carnivals became a regular feature from the 1920s, raising money for the hospital and other charities.

THE GROWING TOWN

In 1842 Southend became a parish separate from Prittlewell. However, it was not until 1866 that the town had its own local Board of Health – the Southend Local Board – whose duty it was to control matters of planning, including roads, health and sanitation and education. The board's members were elected from among the local landowners and ratepayers (basically the town's businessmen) and were responsible, ultimately, to the general Board of Health, established by Act of Parliament in 1848.

By 1892 the population of the town had increased to about 12,000 and, in that year, Southend achieved municipal borough status. Twenty-two years later, in 1914, county borough status was awarded. This status remained with the town until 1974 when, under local government reorganization, Southend reverted to being an ordinary borough. At the time of writing, there is a possibility of the town regaining its former unitary authority status.

Southend's rapid growth from a small watering place of the mid-nineteenth century to the largest town in Essex by the mid-twentieth century is illustrated in this section, which covers such topics as housing and housing estates, hotels, special events and public buildings.

St John's church, *c.* 1880. This was built so that the people of the growing settlement of Southend should not have such a long journey to the parish church. It was completed in 1842, when Southend was granted parish status.

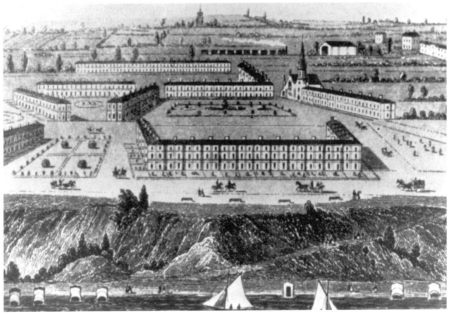

An artist's impression of Clifftown, Southend's first planned housing estate, *c.* 1855. It was built on land leased to the railway contractors Peto, Brassey and Betts. Built by Lucas Brothers, the scheme was completed by about 1860.

Southend, 1875. Even at this date Southend was still quite small. The town was distinctly divided into an upper (new) town to the west, and the old (lower) town to the east, stretching along the seafront and up Southchurch Avenue (the old Southend Lane), with Thames Farm to the east. Here, Clifftown is completed, and the Hamlet Estate, to the north of Clifftown, is just being laid out, as is Porters Town, just to the north of Porters. The Middleton Brewery (otherwise known as Lukers Brewery) had only recently moved from Brewery Road (now Southchurch Avenue). Milton Hall was separated from the town of Southend by open countryside and just to the south of the hall, between it and the windmill, was Southend Park, which had a small lake in the south-west corner. It was here that cricket was played in the summer, hence the name of the local public house.

The Victoria Hospital, Southend, *c.* 1900. The hospital was built on the east side of Warrior Square. The foundation stone was laid in August 1887, the year of the queen's jubilee, and the hospital was opened in May the following year.

Construction of the Municipal Buildings, *c.* 1895. In 1894 Southend Council agreed to the building of 'technical schools' adjoining the Southend Institute buildings, in Clarence Road. These new schools were to include municipal rooms and the whole complex was called the Municipal Buildings. (Reproduced by courtesy of the Essex Record Office (D/DS 229/7))

A crowd paying its respects to Queen Victoria, on her death in 1901. The statue was erected in 1897 to commemorate her diamond jubilee. It was paid for by the mayor, Alderman Bernard Wiltshire Tollhurst, and was made of carrera limestone in the studios of Wm. Swimbourne in Rome.

The Hotel Metropole under construction, *c.* 1900. The hotel was opened in 1904 and was later renamed the Palace Hotel. It is still a prominent feature of the town.

Hotel Victoria, *c.* 1905. Opened in 1899, the hotel boasted a large restaurant, banqueting hall, coffee and smoking rooms, assembly hall and ninety bedrooms. It was certainly Southend's luxury hotel and was most famous for its turkish baths.

The Queen's Hotel also opened in 1899 and had forty-six bedrooms, turkish baths, a roof promenade and a conservatory.

Election posters at Prittlewell, *c.* 1900. Southend won municipal borough status in 1892, when its population had reached about 12,000.

The Municipal College, Victoria Circus, c. 1955. The original Municipal Buildings were
built in Clarence Road (see page 50), as a school and municipal offices. It soon became
apparent that the educational work was suffering from lack of space, and so it was
decided, in 1897, to erect 'new schools and a public gymnasium' in Victoria Avenue. A
competition was held for designs and this was won by H.T. Hare. The schools were
opened in September 1902. At first the schools accepted both boys and girls, but when
the girls left to go to a new school in Boston Avenue, the Victoria Circus premises were
renamed the Southend High School for Boys. It remained so until 1939, when the new
boys' school was opened in Prittlewell Chase. The building then reverted to its original
name of Municipal or Technical College.

This large and impressive house was built on the south-west corner of Victoria Avenue and Great Eastern Avenue just after the turn of the century, and was called Colombier, which is French for dovecote. It was owned by Josiah Sellar, a local timber merchant.

The Central Library, early this century. This building, also designed by H.T. Hare, was opened in 1906. It was Southend's first free public library and was built at the southern end of Victoria Avenue. The project was financed by Andrew Carnegie, at a cost of about £8,000.

Thorpe Bay from the air, mid-1930s. In this photograph the eastern part of the town is still largely undeveloped. However, it wasn't very long before most of this area was swallowed up by the developers responding to the ever growing need for housing.

The Home and Atlantic fleet, 1909. The navy honoured the town when it moored off Southend. The event was described in the *Southend and Westcliff Graphic* as 'the mightiest assembly of war vessels the world has ever seen'.

Fleet decorations, 1909. 'From end to end the Borough will be dressed with flags and bunting. In the principal streets Venetian masts and triumphal arches, strings of Chinese lanterns and multi-coloured fairy lights. . . .'

King George V's visit to Southend, 1921. The king came to view the yacht *Britannia* during yachting week. Here the cavalcade proceeds down Victoria Avenue, opposite Earnsbrake's house, which, by 1925, was to be completely enveloped by the Victoria Arcade shopping complex.

The building of the Chalkwell Hall Estate, *c.* 1905. The first part of the estate had been built in the early years of the present century and a description of it stated 'how charming is the situation and . . . the arrangement of the estate is not liable to serious disturbance . . . '.

The Devonshire Estate nearing completion at Eastwood. The council minutes for 1935–6 record that 'the names for intended new streets were approved: Brendon Way, Lympstone Close and Bideford Close'.

The building of the Argyll Flats at the
top of the cliffs, Westcliff, 1937.

Southend needs houses, *c.* 1925. An advertisement of Davey & Armitage, timber
merchants. The photograph was taken by Alfred Padgett.

Cuckoo Corner, 1923. This photograph, taken by the Borough Engineer's Department, shows the area of Cuckoo Corner, looking south towards Prittlewell Church. The new arterial road was being laid out at this time. (Reproduced by courtesy of the Essex Record Office (D/BC 1/4/10/15/5))

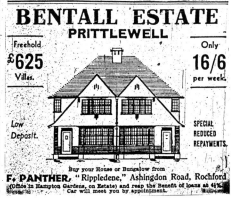

Advertisements for the Bentall Estate, 1935. The 1930s was a period of great house building in Southend, and especially in the mock-Tudor style.

Section Five

SHOPS AND
SHOPPING

The earliest shops in Southend were those serving the needs of the inhabitants of the riverside settlement – mostly fishermen, farmers, and their families, public house proprietors, blacksmiths and other tradespeople. The shops, such as existed, were situated mostly along the seafront, now Marine Parade. When Clifftown was developed, as part of Southend's 'New Town', it had its own shopping centre, in Nelson Street.

The High Street was not originally a shopping road; this came later, from the 1870s onwards, when the first shops were built at the southern end, near the seafront. It was not until the 1890s that the High Street was completed as the town's main shopping thoroughfare. From the 1880s many of the town's principal shops were in the hands of a few families, who were to become household names: Dowsett, R.A. Jones, Garons, Martin (Schofield and Martin), and Brightwell, Havens, Ravens and Keddie to mention but a few. In later years other family firms became prominent, among them Dixons, a familiar sight at Victoria Circus. As the principal members of these families died or retired, and as costs mounted, some of the familiar names disappeared from our High Street and other shopping areas.

Nelson Street, *c.* 1865. When Clifftown was laid out in the late 1850s, the only shops in the New Town were here. Today, although the street is largely unchanged, the only shop front to remain intact is the last in this row, at the northern end. Here were to be found: F. Garon, ironmonger; George Cooch, grocer, and William Griffin, grocer; Alfred Harrison, linen draper; James Lawrence, fancy repository; Chas Taylor, stationer; and John Voisey, cabinet maker.

Godward's shop in the High Street. One of the first shops to occupy this road, Godward supplied horticultural needs. He described himself as 'The Royal Horticultural Establishment', having been patronised by H.R.H. Princess Louise.

The High Street, *c.* 1870. On the left is the small house of Attridge, on the corner of Clifftown Road. In the background is the chimney of Luker's Brewery. The site of the brewery is still remembered in Luker Road.

Thomas Dowsett's shop, July 1881. It was situated on the corner of High Street and Alexandra Street. In 1892 Dowsett became Southend's first mayor. This picture, and the one below, were taken when the Essex Agricultural Show visited the town.

Looking up High Street, towards Dowsett's shop, July 1881. These shops, with rooms above, were built in the early 1870s by Thomas Dowsett. In 1874 Dowsett sought permission from the local board to build a new road called Market Place at the back of these shops.

William Sharpe's shop, *c.* 1898. He, with J.T.S. Dyer, founded St Ann's builders' merchants in about 1896. They manufactured metal window and door frames, stained glass and wrought ironwork.

Christmas decorations in the High Street, *c.* 1905. On the left is Dowsett's shop.

The shop of Robert Arthur Jones, *c.* 1890. R.A. Jones took over an existing jeweller's business in the High Street and quickly became the 'County Jewellers'. It was probably the best known of all the High Street shops, not least because of 'Jones' Clock', which projected from the store.

The High Street, *c.* 1900. To the right is Tipper's Hotel and Restaurant. This was described in 1899 as the 'Southend Mecca for Single Men – A Haven of Luxury'. It had a dining room for 350.

Southend High Street, 1900. This view, taken by G. Dawson, shows the eastern side of the High Street, comprising two banks and several shops, including Tipper's Restaurant. Today the whole of this area of the High Street is covered by the Royals Shopping Centre.

The High Street, c. 1910. Here you can see Jones' Clock on the right, just beyond Edwards' Tobacconists. By this date the whole of the High Street had been developed as shops, many with domestic accommodation above.

Collins opened his first dairy here in Sutton Road in 1911. In 1914, at the outbreak of the First World War, he sold out to Howard's Dairies. He restarted his business in 1922 in Albert Road and, in the 1960s, moved to the Marine Park Dairies.

Havens was established in Hamlet Court Road in 1901, when this picture was taken. The original building was just single storey, as here, but later the shop was completely rebuilt on the same site.

Another view of Havens, *c*. 1920.

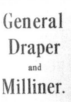

Advertisements from the local newspapers, 1920s. At this time, and up to the 1950s and '60s, most businesses were in the hands of long-established family firms.

Garons, in the High Street, 1912. H. Garon opened his first shop at 64 High Street in 1885. By 1947 Garons owned thirty-seven shops, two factories, a bakery and a hotel. (Reproduced by courtesy of the Essex Record Office (D/BC 1/4/10/18/52))

Schofield & Martin stores, 22 Hamlet Court Road, Westcliff, *c.* 1950. The first store was started by Albert (later Sir Albert) Martin with Mr Schofield in 1892. After four years Martin bought out his partner, and later opened other branches all over the borough and beyond.

Keddies, Southend High Street, mid-1950s. The firm was started by G.J. Keddie in 1894; he bought two shops in the High Street. His son, Arthur Maitland Keddie, expanded the business and became an international authority on window dressing.

Inside the Victoria Arcade, late 1960s. Quite incorrectly called by almost everybody the Talza Arcade (which was just one part of the complex), it opened in 1925. These pictures were taken on the last day of opening for Laurie Mathews, owner of the Art Shop here. Victoria Arcade was demolished in 1969.

The opening of the new Supa Save store in Warrior Square. This was the town's first supermarket. It occupied the old Essoldo cinema (earlier the Strand) building, which was closed in May 1960.

Section Six

SOUTHEND AT WORK

The earliest industries in Southend were farming and fishing. In the nineteenth century the Milton Hall Brick Company was formed, with its first brickfields in the heart of the town. In the same century Henry Luker established his brewery (in Brewery Road, and then the High Street). Several mineral water firms were also founded, responding to the growing demands of tourists and residents. At the turn of the century, following the demands of visitors, Southend's first rock factory went into production.

Serving the local resident population were, of course, the milkmen (such as Howard's Dairies with its own herds of cows), the local steam laundries (such as Albany and Elton) and suppliers of building materials, to mention but a few. Others at hand to serve the local population were the firemen – volunteers at first – and the police force.

In 1892 Southend was created a municipal borough, and elected its first mayor from among the members of the borough's predecessor – the Southend Local Board, which had been formed in 1866.

'Kit' Lester, the unofficial Town Crier of Southend, *c.* 1875. He died in 1901 and his hand bell survives in Southend Central Museum. His real name was William Lester and he worked from the top of Pier Hill to Victoria Circus, announcing anything from lost watches to houses for sale. This portrait was taken by the Rembrandt Studios in the High Street.

Thomas Dowsett, the first mayor of Southend, *c.* 1892. The town had been created a municipal borough in 1892 and chose Dowsett, one of its leading businessmen, to be its chief citizen.

Southend Fire Brigade, 1891. A volunteer fire brigade was formed in the town in 1877 under the auspices of the Southend Local Board. The brigade was reorganised in 1878 and Mr G. Lingwood, manager of the Water Works, was put in charge. He remained chief officer until 1881.

A fire at Southend, July 1900. The *Southend Standard* reported: 'The excitement was intense; High Street, Weston Road and Clarence Street were quickly blocked and, as the flames literally devoured the offices opposite the post office, the wildest rumours spread with regard to alleged ravages.'

The milkmen prepare to make their rounds, 1911. Mr Collins is standing far right. Milk churns and milk measures are well to the fore.

An auctioneer in Southend by G. Dawson, September 1900. Unfortunately I know very little about this photograph. It is described as an 'auctioneer in the street selling grapes'. The photograph was taken near Alexandra Street, and Schofield & Martin's store is in the background.

The pier diver, *c.* 1890. Mr Watson is wearing the diver's suit and Tom Culham, who worked on the pier extension, is holding the helmet. The diver's suit was kept in a shed in Culham's garden.

Laying tram lines at Victoria Circus, *c.* 1900. Looking south down the High Street, on the left is the canopy of the Hotel Victoria. Note all the trees.

Working on the tramlines at the Cricketers, 1908. This photograph was taken to record the progress being made in doubling the tram tracks. (Reproduced by courtesy of the Essex Record Office (D/BC 1/4/10/9/20))

A photograph taken towards the end of the use of horse-drawn milk floats by Howard's Dairies. H.G. Howard began his dairy business at Folly Farm, in Leigh. In 1967 the dairy merged with another local company, Eccles Creamery Ltd.

St Ann's, early this century. This is a view of the workshops where door and window frames and other metal goods were made.

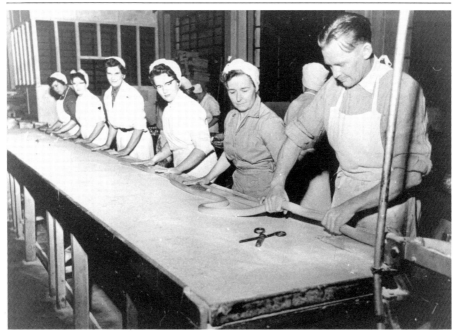

George & Sons, 'The home of Southend rock', 1960s. The ingredients for the rock (and sweets) were mixed in the large steam boiling pans and then the $1\frac{1}{4}$ hundredweight of sugar was rolled out to 1,680 feet.

In this stall and shop which stood opposite the Kursaal in Southchurch Avenue, Mr and Mrs Payne and their family hired out bath chairs and push chairs, served teas and dinners, and offered a wash and brush-up service. The photograph dates from about 1925.

E.K. Cole's factory (Ekco), behind Priory Park, *c.* 1936. Staff are inspecting television tubes ready for assembly. In 1935 Ekco reached an agreement with Scophony for the manufacture of televisions. The company had a world-wide reputation.

At Ekco, assembling radios on the factory floor, *c.* 1935. Eric Cole and Mr Verralls began a partnership in 1925 to manufacture wirelesses in Leigh. In 1930 the factory moved to Southend and, by 1932, was employing about 2,000 people.

Section Seven

TRANSPORT

Before the advent of the railway the only means of transport to Southend was by boat or by horse or horse-drawn vehicle. Regular stage services plied the route from London to Southend from the closing years of the eighteenth century. There were also regular paddle steamer services down the Thames from the early years of the nineteenth century.

Southend did not expand to any great extent, either as a holiday resort or place of residence, until the opening of the rail link with London in 1856. The opening of the second line, in 1889, from Liverpool Street, led to fierce competition and low fares. In the early 1890s the return fare to London was just 1s. 6d. Hardly surprising, then, that Southend became the playground for the East End.

In 1901 the first tramway routes were opened in Southend, and, in 1925, the first 'trackless' trolleys. The first cars were seen in Southend just after the turn of the century. These were closely followed by motor buses and the early charabancs. This new mode of transport necessitated the building of new roads. The Southend arterial road – the A127 – was opened in 1925.

The *London Belle* off Southend, *c.* 1905. This was just one of the many paddle steamers to visit Southend. The *Medway Queen*, *Crested Eagle* and *Royal Daffodil* are among some of the others which took passengers to Herne Bay, Clacton, London, Margate and elsewhere.

A paddle steamer leaving Southend from the newly opened Prince George extension, *c.* 1929.

Southend Central station, 1860. When this photograph was taken it was the only railway station in the town. The line to Southend was completed in 1856, by Peto, Brassey and Betts, and Mr Stride was the manager of the line.

Peter Trigg's coach at Southend, *c.* 1895. Peter Trigg was the principal owner of horse-drawn passenger vehicles at the end of the last century. Before the tram and motor car, and later the omnibus services, a horse-drawn bus service was essential. Trigg's stables were near Luker's Brewery.

The first trams to enter Warrior Square, 11 May 1921. These were among the last new cars to be bought by the corporation from Brush, and were the first to have enclosed top decks. (Reproduced by courtesy of the Essex Record Office (D/BC 1/4/10/9/154))

The Victoria Circus tramway office, *c.* 1910. It was built by Messrs W. MacFarlane & Co. of Glasgow, from 1909 to 1910.

Destined for Leigh, car 54 advertises the Kursaal, 1920s. The tram is pictured here on Thorpe Hall Boulevard, which was opened to traffic in 1914.

Southend-on-Sea & District omnibus, *c.* 1906. In 1906 the Southend-on-Sea & District Motor Omnibus Co. ran three double-decker buses between Southend, Hadleigh, Rochford and Shoebury. The corporation ran an experimental bus service, but abandoned the idea in 1916.

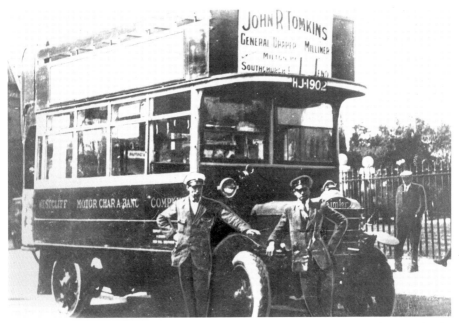

The Westcliff-on-Sea Motor Charabanc Company began to operate a bus service in 1920. The first route was from the High Street to Hamlet Court Road. Later they were renamed Westcliff-on-Sea Motor Services and operated over most of south-east Essex.

Southend's first trolley bus, Victoria Circus, 1925. The buses were much more versatile than trams, because they did not need tracks. They were, however, less comfortable to drive – note the solid tyres. This vehicle was taken out of service in 1933.

An early car in Southend, *c*. 1905. On 6 March 1902 an article in the local paper stated that 'There are two classes of motor car driver who use the streets of Southend and neighbourhood. Some progress steadily and others are veritable Jehus, for they are feared through furious driving, (at) a speed of fourteen miles an hour.'

Charabancs were becoming ever more popular in the 1920s. A report in the *Southend Standard* stated: 'The popularity of the char-a-banc does not lessen, and the wear and tear of the roads increases. Quite what the evolution of the new movement will be it is difficult to predict, but it is evident local authorities will have to take greater powers to control, so that they may order the routes, restrain the unnecessary noises which accompany the career of these vehicles, and generally preserve to townspeople their traffic rights. . . . Char-a-banc motoring has come to stay, and we best serve our interests by welcoming the passengers.'

A very famous name in Southend: one of Garon's horse-drawn delivery vans photographed possibly in the 1920s.

George & Sons was the first company in the town to have its own delivery vans, seen here in 1924.

Looking east along Prince Avenue, 1953. The '50s were probably the heyday of the day trip by coach. At this time the town became absolutely full of coaches, especially the Kursaal and Seaway coach parks, as Londoners poured in to see the lights and enjoy the amusements the seafront had to offer.

Section Eight

SOUTHEND AT WAR

Southend witnessed the first air raid on this country during the First World War. Several incendiary and explosive bombs fell on the town in May 1915, causing considerable damage and understandable alarm and, in August 1917, thirty-two people were killed in an air raid. During the war the Palace Hotel was used as a hospital for sick and wounded servicemen, and volunteers were called for to serve in the civic watch and street fire patrols.

Defensive measures in preparation for the Second World War were well under way by 1938. Local Home Guard units and an Air Raid Precautions committee were formed. The pier and Royal Terrace were taken over by the Admiralty and, in June 1940, Southend schoolchildren were evacuated to a number of destinations in Derbyshire and Northamptonshire; the airport became a fighter drome, and troops were billeted all over the town. By April 1940 17,000 Anderson shelters had been allocated to the borough. By 16 July in the same year the town had been declared an evacuation area.

From 1944 the town's council was planning the building of temporary housing on several sites in the borough, to replace the damaged properties. This saw the introduction of the 'prefab'.

SOUTHEND STANDARD"

Air Raid Supplement

THURSDAY, MAY 13, 1915.

You English We Have Come
& Well come again soon
Kill or Cure

The front page from the *Southend Standard* special supplement, reporting on the first air raid on the town, May 1915. A message dropped from one of the Zeppelins read 'You English We Have Come and Well Come Again Soon, German.'

Bomb damage to a house in West Road, 10 May 1915. The raid occurred on the previous night, the bombs being dropped by a Zeppelin (LZ 38) commanded by Hauptmann Erich Linnarz.

Damage to a butcher's shop, Hamlet Court Road, Westcliff, after the same raid. The government were particularly annoyed by detailed reporting of the damage caused by the enemy.

Standing guard over fallen bombs. 'An unexploded bomb at Victoria Corner, Southend, and the men who recovered it.' (*Southend Standard*, 9 May 1915)

Queen Mary's Royal Naval Hospital, Palace Hotel, *c.* 1915. The hotel was converted to hospital use between August and October 1914, when it opened, and cared for both British and Belgian sick and wounded. From March 1917 only sailors were treated there.

Raising funds for the hospital, *c.* 1916. Collections and special events were organised by the Friends of the hospital. These included 'rose' days and gift days.

Wounded soldiers at the hospital, *c.* 1915. Since it opened, the hospital had, up to March 1917, treated 169 Belgian soldiers, 3,382 British soldiers and 744 British sailors. The number of beds had been increased from 220 to 350.

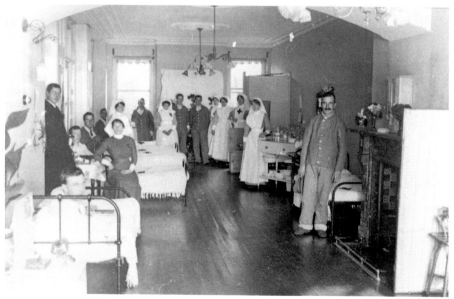

One of the wards in the hospital. At one end of the converted Palace Hotel were the winter gardens, which were now used as an operating theatre. Miss Finnemore, who had been a nurse in South Africa (in the Boer War), was appointed matron in charge of thirty nurses.

This is the bomb which fell on Mrs Anstill's house & killed his 2 little birds. He sent this P.C. to the Kaiser, but it was returned marked "Not Deliverable 'Enemy' Country." This bomb was dropped just a few yards away from our house on the occasion of the 2nd visit of the Zeppelin. Thus we escaped a second time very narrowly.

Saw the 2 little birds directly they were killed. Poor Mrs A. seemed awfully upset about their deaths.

VICTIMS OF AIR RAID
SOUTHEND-ON-SEA
26. MAY. 1915.

Two pages from a scrapbook compiled by Mrs Emily Gilbert, who visited the hospital throughout the war. She helped wounded and dying men brought from the battlefields of France and Gallipoli. In return, the soldiers gave her souvenirs and first-hand accounts of the fighting. The book includes many photographs of the hospital and its patients.

Sitting down is on "Vaughan, 2nd Dennis, 2nd Rifle Brigade

4454 Pte H. Vaughan. 2nd Lancashire Fus: gassed at Ypres on the 2nd May 1915. and then inflicted excruciating torture on the nursing staff by gassing, gassing, gassing. till he departed this 22nd May 1915. ("Snore")

A 'downed' Zeppelin in the Thames estuary, off Southend, 10 April 1916.

German prisoners arrive in Southend, November 1914. The first German prisoners to arrive in Southend were escorted by armed guard to three prison ships moored off Southend Pier. They were the Cunard liners *Saxonia*, *Ivernia* and *Royal Edward*.

Southend High School for Boys, 8 June 1940. It was among the first buildings to be bombed during the Second World War. The caption on the photograph read: 'Extensive damage was caused to a school in the area by a high explosive bomb dropped during the raid on Tuesday.'

Local children waiting to be evacuated to new homes, *c*. 1940. Evacuation of children from Southend began in June 1940. The Southend town clerk reported that the Minister of Home Security made an order on 16 July declaring the borough to be an evacuation area.

'A further batch of 500 Southend schoolchildren were evacuated on Tuesday morning and the above picture shows them at the LNER station, 25 June 1940.' This quotation, and those in subsequent captions, is taken from the reverse of the original.

'They had left their homes but they were smiling as they went.'

Girls from Southend High School for Girls being marched towards the railway station, June 1940. Together with girls from Sacred Heart School, St Helens and London Road Schools, these children were evacuated to Mansfield.

Southend railway station, February 1941. 'Coaches were damaged when a bomb fell on a railway station on Tuesday night.'

Manners Way, August 1940. This newly built block of flats and shops suffered a direct hit towards the end of August.

Victoria Circus, August 1942. 'The Leigh Section of the Home Guard gave a demonstration of machine gun work on Monday, at the "Guns for Attack" exhibition at Victoria Circus, Southend.'

Southend aerodrome, April 1942. A Spitfire is ready to take off.

At the aerodrome, 25 April 1942. 'The cannon of a Spitfire being tested at the butts at an RAF fighter station in Essex.'

A wrecked plane, Fox Hall Farm, March 1943. The censor has stamped on the back of the photograph 'Not to be Published'.

Mobile canteen, August 1943. This served cups of tea after an air raid.

Damaged houses, Colemans Avenue, November 1941.

Southend police station, Alexandra Street, *c.* 1939. Brick wall protection is being built in front of the police station.

Southend aerodrome, August 1940. A Dornier crashed on the aerodrome and was being carefully guarded.

The Home Guard rifle range, July 1942. Brigadier W. Garden Roe MC fired the first shot after opening the range at Prittlewell.

Cumberland Avenue, November 1940. 'A bomb fell in the garden of this house during a raid on south-east England early on Tuesday morning. The shelter was unoccupied and the people in the house escaped.'

Bomb damage to the High Street, 1942. Considerable damage was done to the London Hotel and adjacent properties (see pages 66–67 for earlier photographs of the High Street).

Clearing up after the raid.

London Road, Westcliff. 'A German bomb helps the Spitfire Fund. This novel collecting box is the idea of the wardens of post 402.'

A Czech squadron, Southend aerodrome. 'This squadron has put in some excellent work.'

Southend Home Guard band, at the bandstand on the cliffs, *c*. 1940.

A policeman is now ready for anything! This is Mr Shreeve, of Hamlet Court Road, who served as a Special Constable during the war. He was photographed in about 1940.

An 'ack-ack' gun, probably on Southend Pier. The pier was a lifeline for the convoys assembling in the Thames, and its defence was essential.

Southend Pier, November 1939. Mr A.J. Green (left) and a colleague on duty with the Observer Corps, on the end of the pier.

Looking for the nearest ARP shelter, 1943.

Mr Payne emerges unscathed from his Anderson shelter in Southchurch Avenue.

THE CHANGING
FACE OF SOUTHEND

The centre of Southend had undergone a very gradual evolution from the 1890s to the 1950s. The principal buildings at the heart of the town – the Municipal College, the library, the northern end of the High Street, including the Hotel Victoria – had all been completed by the first few years of this century. Trams had also been introduced at this time, and the pattern of overhead tram wires at Victoria Circus gave it the name of 'Cobweb Corner'. The most recent of the buildings in this area was the Victoria Arcade, opened in 1925.

Things were to change quite dramatically in the 1960s. As in most other towns, this decade saw a sweeping away of all that was old, to be replaced by the new architecture, and new concepts of shopping resulted in the construction of the pedestrian precinct. In this, the final, section, we take a glimpse at the recent past in not-so-old photographs. Many will remember the earlier scenes in this section with great affection. I leave it up to you, the reader, to compare the old with the new.

Victoria Circus from the air, 1960. At the top of the photograph, just to the left of centre, are the trees surrounding the library. At the top centre is the Victoria railway station, with buses parked in front; one is just pulling out into Victoria Avenue. The Victoria Arcade is prominent on the right of the picture, with Earnsbrake's house near its bottom corner. Opposite this, towards the bottom of the photograph, is the Hotel Victoria. The flat roof of Dixons can be found on the opposite side of the High Street. The most prominent landmark is, of course, the Municipal College.

Looking up the High Street from over the pier, *c.* 1955. How things have changed! The pier buildings have gone, and the area in the middle of the photograph is now occupied by the Royals Shopping Centre.

A tree-lined Victoria Avenue, *c.* 1965. Apart from St Mary's church on the right, the only tall building is the block of new flats (Cecil Court) opposite.

Widening the Victoria Avenue into a dual carriageway, *c.* 1970. The picture is taken from the Civic Centre, and shows the bowling green; by this time the houses on the right-hand side of the road in the previous photograph had been demolished.

Victoria Circus, Whit Sunday, 1953. On the left, with troughs full of flowers, is Dixons; beyond Dixons is the Municipal College on the other side of the circus. On the east side (the right), can be seen the Victoria Arcade, with Garons Tea Shop on the corner, and beyond this is the library. In the foreground is a bus of the City Coach Company, which was the major coach company transporting passengers between London and Southend. Behind the coach there are three double-decker trolley buses. It is no wonder that Victoria Circus was once known as 'Cobweb Corner'. In the distance is the tree-lined Victoria Avenue, long before the building of office blocks.

The Gaumont Cinema. Opened as the Hippodrome in 1909 in a building designed by Bertie Crewe, performers included Marie Lloyd, George Robey, Flanagan and Allen, and, later when it became the Gaumont, Norman Wisdom in 'Trouble in Store'. It closed in 1956 and was demolished in 1958.

Talmage Buildings, including what was the Civic News Theatre (here the 'New Vic'), all part of the Victoria Arcade, September 1966.

Looking south down the High Street from Victoria Circus, *c*. 1953. Dixons is on the right and the Hotel Victoria on the left. The town still had many old family firms, among them Dixons, where you could buy almost anything in the clothing and home-furnishing line. On the left side of the road, beyond Hotel Victoria, is just visible the old frontage of Keddies, with flagpoles above.

Victoria Circus, September 1966. The view is from the north-west and shows the Hotel Victoria and Garons Corner.

Virtually the same view, August 1969. The Hotel Victoria has been replaced by the new Barclays Bank. The clock has been removed from Garons Corner.

One end of the temporary footbridge, opposite the side of the Technical College, September 1968. The bridge was erected during the redevelopment of Victoria Circus.

A scene of destruction, August 1969. This photograph was taken during the demolition of the Victoria Arcade. The Technical College is left in total isolation, though it, too, was soon to be demolished.

The temporary footbridge from the railway station, September 1969. It carried pedestrians above the new dual carriageway being constructed below.

The new shopping bridge completed, July 1969. The outdoor escalator is being raised into place.

The new Victoria Circus from the air, *c.* 1970 (compare with page 116). The old Victoria Circus can be seen here in the bottom right-hand corner and the roof of the Municipal College is to the left. Victoria station is centre left.

Acknowledgements

I wish to thank all those people and institutions who have so generously lent me photographs and given permission for their inclusion in this book. In particular I must mention Southend Museums Service, and its curator, Arthur Wright, who generously allowed the use of a very large number of previously unpublished images. The following people also, on many occasions, helped with essential information regarding their photographs, dates, events and personalities.

Ekco Sports and Social Club • Essex Record Office• Essex Libraries
G.J. Keddies & Sons • John Lewis Partnership • Mr Byford • L. Mathews
Mr Leggett • Frank Allen • M. Davies • P. Culham • G. Briggs • Mr Scanes
W. Wren • G. Collins • Mr Yeatts • G. Williams
J. Heiser • J. Porter • J. Stumpke • Mrs N. Deacon
Mrs J. Moriarty • Mrs O. Green • Mrs Payne • Mrs E. Hogsflesh
Mrs J. Sutcliffe • Mrs H. Feather • Mrs M. Thompson
Mrs P. Knight • Ms A. Scarrott • R. Havens • Southend Museums Service
Southend Council (Borough Engineers Department).

BRITAIN IN OLD PHOTOGRAPHS

To order any of these titles please telephone 01453 731114

ALDERNEY

Alderney: A Second Selection, *B Bonnard*

BEDFORDSHIRE

Bedfordshire at Work, *N Lutt*

BERKSHIRE

Maidenhead, *M Hayles & D Hedges*
Around Maidenhead, *M Hayles & B Hedges*
Reading, *P Southerton*
Reading: A Second Selection, *P Southerton*
Sandhurst and Crowthorne, *K Dancy*
Around Slough, *J Hunter & K Hunter*
Around Thatcham, *P Allen*
Around Windsor, *B Hedges*

BUCKINGHAMSHIRE

Buckingham and District, *R Cook*
High Wycombe, *R Goodearl*
Around Stony Stratford, *A Lambert*

CHESHIRE

Cheshire Railways, *M Hitches*
Chester, *S Nichols*

CLWYD

Clwyd Railways, *M Hitches*

CLYDESDALE

Clydesdale, *Lesmahagow Parish Historical Association*

CORNWALL

Cornish Coast, *T Bowden*
Falmouth, *P Gilson*
Lower Fal, *P Gilson*
Around Padstow, *M McCarthy*
Around Penzance, *J Holmes*
Penzance and Newlyn, *J Holmes*
Around Truro, *A Lyne*
Upper Fal, *P Gilson*

CUMBERLAND

Cockermouth and District, *J Bernard Bradbury*
Keswick and the Central Lakes, *J Marsh*
Around Penrith, *F Boyd*
Around Whitehaven, *H Fancy*

DERBYSHIRE

Derby, *D Buxton*
Around Matlock, *D Barton*

DEVON

Colyton and Seaton, *T Gosling*
Dawlish and Teignmouth, *G Gosling*
Devon Aerodromes, *K Saunders*
Exeter, *P Thomas*
Exmouth and Budleigh Salterton, *T Gosling*
From Haldon to Mid-Dartmoor, *T Hall*
Honiton and the Otter Valley, *J Yallop*
Around Kingsbridge, *K Tanner*
Around Seaton and Sidmouth, *T Gosling*
Seaton, Axminster and Lyme Regis, *T Gosling*

DORSET

Around Blandford Forum, *B Cox*
Bournemouth, *M Colman*
Bridport and the Bride Valley, *J Burrell & S Humphries*
Dorchester, *T Gosling*
Around Gillingham, *P Crocker*

DURHAM

Darlington, *G Flynn*
Darlington: A Second Selection, *G Flynn*
Durham People, *M Richardson*
Houghton-le-Spring and Hetton-le-Hole, *K Richardson*
Houghton-le-Spring and Hetton-le-Hole:
A Second Selection, *K Richardson*
Sunderland, *S Miller & B Bell*
Teesdale, *D Coggins*
Teesdale: A Second Selection, *P Raine*
Weardale, *J Crosby*
Weardale: A Second Selection, *J Crosby*

DYFED

Aberystwyth and North Ceredigion,
Dyfed Cultural Services Dept
Haverfordwest, *Dyfed Cultural Services Dept*
Upper Tywi Valley, *Dyfed Cultural Services Dept*

ESSEX

Around Grays, *B Evans*

GLOUCESTERSHIRE

Along the Avon from Stratford to Tewkesbury, *J Jeremiah*
Cheltenham: A Second Selection, *R Whiting*
Cheltenham at War, *P Gill*
Cirencester, *J Welsford*
Around Cirencester, *E Cuss & P Griffiths*
Forest, The, *D Mullin*
Gloucester, *J Voyce*
Around Gloucester, *A Sutton*
Gloucester: From the Walwin Collection, *J Voyce*
North Cotswolds, *D Viner*
Severn Vale, *A Sutton*
Stonehouse to Painswick, *A Sutton*
Stroud and the Five Valleys, *S Gardiner & L Padin*
Stroud and the Five Valleys: A Second Selection,
S Gardiner & L Padin
Stroud's Golden Valley, *S Gardiner & L Padin*
Stroudwater and Thames & Severn Canals,
E Cuss & S Gardiner
Stroudwater and Thames & Severn Canals: A Second
Selection, *E Cuss & S Gardiner*
Tewkesbury and the Vale of Gloucester, *C Hilton*
Thornbury to Berkeley, *J Hudson*
Uley, Dursley and Cam, *A Sutton*
Wotton-under-Edge to Chipping Sodbury, *A Sutton*

GWYNEDD

Anglesey, *M Hitches*
Gwynedd Railways, *M Hitches*
Around Llandudno, *M Hitches*
Vale of Conwy, *M Hitches*

HAMPSHIRE

Gosport, *J Sadden*
Portsmouth, *P Rogers & D Francis*

HEREFORDSHIRE

Herefordshire, *A Sandford*

HERTFORDSHIRE

Barnet, *I Norrie*
Hitchin, *A Fleck*
St Albans, *S Mullins*
Stevenage, *M Appleton*

ISLE OF MAN

The Tourist Trophy, *B Snelling*

ISLE OF WIGHT

Newport, *D Parr*
Around Ryde, *D Parr*

JERSEY

Jersey: A Third Selection, *R Lemprière*

KENT

Bexley, *M Scott*
Broadstairs and St Peter's, *J Whyman*
Bromley, Keston and Hayes, *M Scott*
Canterbury: A Second Selection, *D Butler*
Chatham and Gillingham, *P MacDougall*
Chatham Dockyard, *P MacDougall*
Deal, *J Broady*
Early Broadstairs and St Peter's, *B Wootton*
East Kent at War, *D Collyer*
Eltham, *J Kennett*
Folkestone: A Second Selection, *A Taylor & E Rooney*
Goudhurst to Tenterden, *A Guilmant*
Gravesend, *R Hiscock*
Around Gravesham, *R Hiscock & D Grierson*
Herne Bay, *J Hawkins*
Lympne Airport, *D Collyer*
Maidstone, *I Hales*
Margate, *R Clements*
RAF Hawkinge, *R Humphreys*
RAF Manston, *RAF Manston History Club*
RAF Manston: A Second Selection,
RAF Manston History Club
Ramsgate and Thanet Life, *D Perkins*
Romney Marsh, *E Carpenter*
Sandwich, *C Wanostrocht*
Around Tonbridge, *C Bell*
Tunbridge Wells, *M Rowlands & I Beavis*
Tunbridge Wells: A Second Selection,
M Rowlands & I Beavis
Around Whitstable, *C Court*
Wingham, Adisham and Littlebourne, *M Crane*

LANCASHIRE

Around Barrow-in-Furness, *J Garbutt & J Marsh*
Blackpool, *C Rothwell*
Bury, *J Hudson*
Chorley and District, *J Smith*
Fleetwood, *C Rothwell*
Heywood, *J Hudson*
Around Kirkham, *C Rothwell*
Lancashire North of the Sands, *J Garbutt & J Marsh*
Around Lancaster, *S Ashworth*
Lytham St Anne's, *C Rothwell*
North Fylde, *C Rothwell*
Radcliffe, *J Hudson*
Rossendale, *B Moore & N Dunnachie*

LEICESTERSHIRE

Around Ashby-de-la-Zouch, *K Hillier*
Charnwood Forest, *I Keil, W Humphrey & D Wix*
Leicester, *D Burton*
Leicester: A Second Selection, *D Burton*
Melton Mowbray, *T Hickman*
Around Melton Mowbray, *T Hickman*
River Soar, *D Wix, P Shacklock & I Keil*
Rutland, *T Clough*
Vale of Belvoir, *T Hickman*
Around the Welland Valley, *S Mastoris*

LINCOLNSHIRE

Grimsby, *J Tierney*
Around Grimsby, *J Tierney*
Grimsby Docks, *J Tierney*
Lincoln, *D Cuppleditch*